Because the bullet arrives

The French poet Jean Follain once said, "Guns are the jewelry of men." In Caroline Rash's poems guns can serve as talismans, for both men and women, of desire and love. Her poems have a richness of close attention to detail. Some are vivid speculations about mortality, and affection for those no longer with us. Others celebrate contact with water, contact of body to body, body in contact with the larger world. In Rash's work we hear voices of both struggle and achievement, inspired by close family bonds, and anticipation of new life.

—Robert Morgan, Author of *Dark Energy*

Because the bullet arrives

Caroline Rash

REDHAWK
PUBLICATIONS

Because the bullet arrives

Copyright © 2025 Caroline Rash

All rights reserved. No part of this publication may be reproduced, distributed, or transmitted in any form or by any means, including photocopying, recording, or other electronic or mechanical methods, without the prior written permission of the publisher, except in the case of brief quotations embodied in critical reviews and certain other noncommercial uses permitted by copyright law. For permission requests, write to the publisher, addressed "Attention: Permissions Coordinator," at the address below.

ISBN: 978-1-959346-87-6 (Paperback)

Library of Congress Control Number: 2025933319

Cover Design (Art): Sarah Moore
Book Interior Design: Robert T Canipe

Printed in the United States of America.

First printing 2025.

Redhawk Publications
The Catawba Valley Community College Press
2550 Hwy 70 SE
Hickory NC 28602
https://redhawkpublications.com

For Mom and Dad,

my first and best teachers

TABLE OF CONTENTS

Heirloom	9
Entry wound	10
When the Pentecostal pastor asked	16
Cast	17
My mother watched me in the bath	19
In a time of need	20
Invocation	22
(Sonnets I-VI) The birds are stealing window screens	23
Target practice	29
I swam up the Mississippi and sent this letter back	30
Alignment 1.0	31
Alignment 2.0	32
I'm sitting by Lake Hartwell [that one spot we used to go]	33
The banana tree on Deslonde Street	36
Acknowledgments	37
About the Author	39

Caroline Rash

Heirloom

B still makes Japanese pancakes—egg, flour, water.
She says every culture has a meal like that—two or three ingredients,

a scrounging-in-the-cupboards kind of meal. I think of New Orleans
crawfish boils, how proud everyone is to eat the whole bug, not just

étouffée tail or claw meat, the whole bottom feeder, ditch dweller
that nibbled underwater drifts of flesh like snow. B says they have

more flavor. I never had a taste for it, the hundreds laid out
on a wet wood table with brightly cobbled corn, sausage stumps,

squeezed orb of lemon and black-spotted potatoes, nothing wasted,
nothing wasted—even the unread newspaper soaking up juice.

What we eat becomes a habit. I can't look in their eyes. Unblinking
amber beads, loose claws, under the wide mouth of sky.

Because the bullet arrives

Entry wound

Some note
in the bark
sharpens when
dogs smell blood —

        my love is
        nine years old
        when he hears
        them coming.

His father
and uncle
stand even
and sturdy
as the militia
of trees
ushered into
the sun for
their yield and
he tries to stand

        still himself
        feeling his eyes

Caroline Rash

      ache through
      the sight of
      a new .410
      his first shotgun

which houses
a single shell
of makeshift power,
3 double aughts
he sealed inside
with candle wax
before darkness
puddled and
hardened
around the moon

      now falling,
      bowing
      its gentle
      dawn nod to

men and trees
and dogs, the
shrill and certain
cries close now

Because the bullet arrives

to bursting the
white pine wall —

        if the moon
        shone any
        brighter, deer
        would shadow
        -walk & his feet
        still wiggle
        under his blue
        and white

blanket but
here he is,
unable to crack
a fault line
of black birds
in the broad sky,

        a boy
        a sweet, skinny-
        legged boy with
        eyes dark like
        damp soil
        wondering still

Caroline Rash

if he can have

just

one

minute

when the

buck hurdles

the two-rut

dirt path

        where his father

        softly reminded him

        of buck fever,

        how each boy

        thinks soon as

        the gun stops

        shaking he'll pull —

        it never stops shaking.

The white tail

flits across

his vision

like a lighter's

uncaught flame and

the boy has not

Because the bullet arrives

moved,
the black and
brown and
canine blue
cross his vision
and he can not
move,

          though
          the next
          November,
          sitting on
          an upside-down
          five-gallon bucket
          in a treehouse
          of two-by-fours
          birds-eye
          of the field
          planted soft
          with grass,

he will finally
set
in the quiet
second

Caroline Rash

and send
an iron shock
into the first
buck drawn
by bobbing
doe heads
into the open —

        Look, he's the only one
        I know who believes
        in God; he says

he eats meat
because he's slit
a throat and
watched the
blood run,

        and I think
        that's
        the way
        we love.

When the Pentecostal pastor asked all who wanted to be saved to step forward

I did or didn't—depends which time he asked. Because my mother has seen the end of a burning cigarette ash our driveway in early morning

where my grandfather once stood in quiet tobacco banishment. Because she says I don't have to believe the truth. I've watched her is how I know

to show every night for two years in the fluorescent lobby when you slide towards death, to be there if you are gone before the doctor professes it.

Because sometimes we know before our tongue forms the word. And sometimes a dog howls miles away when her owner shudders and stills.

Mama scooped my brother and me up and ran out of that church before we could go up and sing; she said those people were dancing so hard

the walls shook and she feared they'd fall. She said a woman's gut formed impossible words, senseless, rolling like shadows over the mountain.

And yet—the structure stood while we picked daisies from a square of graves. It could have crumbled. I don't see much need to figure it all out.

I'd rather you, your warm flesh, a human sort of promise. The ventilator breathed & my grandfather's nails turned purple. Each night when she

left, he asked my mother How will you find me? Our questions improve; our reason fades. One time I stayed seated, the other I asked for bread.

Cast

Mother lights a lamp   as we duck to duskdark rooms,
stamp the salt and ice from boots   to puddle and smear
inside the door.   That winter, I thumb   my father's
neglected shelves,   the thick yellow stink of squint-small texts,
my bloody bitten fingers   gently dusting each spine. I like
to think then   about my father's hands,   calloused pink
where his pen rests, fleshing the book,   this creature — father —
thinker of far-off thoughts.   I can only go with him   so far
then   he is alone   with the white box-fan blades,
back ache   canyon deep,   and we must quiet
for he is healing,   but we are children,   unable always
to bend limbs   and tiptoe along shelves. The earth
warms slowly,   Mother wipes grease   on her
threadbare jeans   and sends us out —   J to poke
a thin stick   at the trash bin garter snake,   me to pick
tightrope toes   barefoot   along the stone wall.
This is where   I find the fossil   embedded in a blonde
rock, winking   with mica from our creek.   I fold myself
down and see   a many-limbed mindless spine, armored bug
— I am afraid   to touch it.   Soaping dishes, Mother
removes her wedding ring   to sink-side eye-height.   I am
reminded of my treasure then   and tug her sleeve,   but
no one believes when I finger trilobite in the encyclopedia,

Because the bullet arrives

its ribbed carbon body by then a lost rock. And I can't imagine
now   why I set it down,   but I was child unable to hold
one thing.   Still, my belief in the old sea dweller
flowed   ocean currents through our home,   the pale sky
heavied with water pressure, and I swam   through tiger lilies
to reach   the toolshed,   gasp air and stir bottom feeders
with light beams   cast from my submarine's   foggy portal.
From that dusty sill   I waved to my father when he emerged
in late spring to hoe-halve an arrowhead snake. Its flesh stank
through May;   by June, only its   moonwhite spine remained.

Caroline Rash

my mother watched me in the bath

and the first time
I saw through
her fleshy peach
bra I thought
the two dark
spots meant that
she'd been shot

Because the bullet arrives

in a time of need

will you

love my

flesh where

it folds

where it

freckles

and rusts

rice-paper

thin, stir

orbits

with milk

in our

coffee,

carve our

letters

in wet

logs heavy

with april?

you're

so brave

is why.

I like to

watch you

Caroline Rash

wrench the
garden
knob with
one hand
and stick
up to wrist
in trickle.
I want
to waste
water
like that.

Because the bullet arrives

Invocation

Bring the storm, please, bring the rain.

A kettle whistles, ginger tea steam
curls and fogs a window. The dog winds
in circles like a watch, nose to haunch,
nose to haunch. Impending, thin
tremor of air like insect wings,

bring it all down, please, bring the rain.

The tub is filled, dishes done.
Porch steps cool my bare feet taking in
the weak and pretty flowers; my eyes scan
the sky still open and placid as a petal.
Such a day must surely soak and tear,

so bring the storm, bring the rain.

I ask my neighbor, a stranger,
Where is the rain? [I could bike back
to the gallery where I left you
in this sunlight. I could run yet into
the street with a mania of questions.]

Sonnets I-VI: The Birds

I. The birds are stealing window screens

The birds are stealing window screens—at first,
a plucked trellis by the dining room, now our bed.
Allowed our ferns and rose of Sharon, they
approached, unwove the wire for bedding nest.

And, yes, I hung a feeder, yes, I filled it
with cracked corn and millet, I quit wetting dark
the ferns and laughed to catch on camera four
fuzzy, bobbing heads last spring, their frantic arc

to nearby oak. From garden to gutter to fern
the birds advance, unravel, until a hole as big as
a fist has formed—we watch through humid glass.
You ask what we owe them, then take it back,

nail the fern steady against wind and prowling cats.
In your left eye, something pale and mottled cracks.

Because the bullet arrives

II. And after the clutch of pearls we sheltered in

And after the clutch of pearls we sheltered in
our fern breaks open, I raise the screen-
less window, make a hole into our home—
we're not a ship, I say, we won't sink beneath

the weight of fresh air. In doing so, the TV
reflection's gone, gone that rolling credit, the fi-
nal score replaced by life ignored: orchid, moth,
impatient raptor asking me to step aside. I

say welcome: take the screen, the fern, the feed,
the mail, a toothbrush, old gray sock for nest.
And when the trees are full, perhaps they'll stay,
track tiny prints in mantel dust. Oh darling, let's

allow it! Cracked egg in your work boots, shell shard
and hungry mouth in the lace of my top drawer.

III. The birds are in our house now

The birds are in our house now, so I name
them. First, by asking finch or sparrow, et cetera.
Robins are obvious, jays and cardinals too. The rest?
I'm not an ornithologist. Guests. Unguessed

become their calls: whistler, whinny, band
of babblers born in a burned-out lamp.
I come to know these better than the Latinate;
I watch them closer, I inspect their shit and

ask if the cherry chroma's blood or berry.
Our bin's a nest, our stove a robin's home.
The washer's taken, so we soap our shirts in rain.
A farewell transmission through your phone

says crows took the capitol, Fast Cash is on fire;
we're laughing when our last batteries die.

Because the bullet arrives

IV. Come dream with me the walls were trumpeted

Come dream with me the walls were trumpeted
down, rubbled, plucked, and all the deeds that man
mistook for happiness are void. We stopped paying
bills, watch mail gutter-gather, county trash cans

accept no more refuse. Neighbors refuse to leave
and shoot at stray cats, blue jays from fuel-less
cars—pity their decaying half-lives, death
arrived before they own their debt. We tread

debris that shines like shells, break trail by
absurd stumble, listen for northbound cries
of geese soaring surely in such dark. They say:
Have you heard the good news? City lights

died back like August grass. But I forgot the path,
the constellations, and there's no one left to ask.

V. I perch on the useless powerline

I perch on the useless powerline where we
relearned to feed, how to push the air beneath
us, shoulder clear of purse strap, neck free
of collar. One by one, we slip into the

woods. You must go alone, six crows call,
though you'll find your way again to one
another soon, back into your home—if
you go now, if you take less than you can

carry. We return to ash and cracked pavement,
fern and weed and lodgepole peeking through,
watch this spring's clutch in rose of Sharon as
their mother husks and tongues a kernel. We too

want so much from so little, pick and press
soft thumbs to shell, suck seed, toss the rest.

Because the bullet arrives

VI. And so much bounty's sewn inside

And so much bounty's sewn inside a hand-me-
down jacket as children slip into another
country, stepping lightly over ruins, stock-
piles of unfired weapons. A blue, southern

song, northside moss their grizzled guide. You
and I and all the birds wait for their arrival.
I sleep the soiled bed with you on creek-
cool stones, remember how to breathe, lie

still and pray. Somewhere an old woman, face
mottled like an egg, dreamed this decade:
a dark, settled puddle. The steam rising, flight
of fallen things. As humans do, we may yet

conceive a child, believe her light, free: tie her
two shoes as she flies out the door to morning.

Target practice

On Sunday morning we step into the wild yellow field behind
his father's empty house. Our foot-bellies balk at rocks

we've grown estranged from as we cut a barefoot trail, ignore
late summer clouds crowding the sun. I lose my clothes piece

by piece, and he discloses a ladder rung of collarbone, the hole
in the center of his chest, sunken and flanked by muscle,

as though he survived a great blast. He carries a pistol,
sixteen bullets, and one silver beer can to prop on the shoulders

of a fallen and mossed tree. He tells me to shoot first since he
won't miss; so I do, and he doesn't, and the can's pierced

and crushed while we lie on the earth, a bit drunk. The cradle
of his chest like a bird bath slowly fills with rain, and we're still

in no rush. Some love is lost a little at a time, some vacates
the premises overnight. I wonder which way ours will flee.

Between the spent can and my T-shirt tugged back over
my head, I learn how his heart sleeps untenanted again.

Because the bullet arrives

I swam up the Mississippi and sent this letter back

The last time
I touched you

my hand came
back black tarred

with bloody shoe-
shine feathers,

because every
morning pulled

us to the earth
and because I

could not step
for fear of

causing a flood
in Tokyo. And still,

when the wind
set me down

somewhere in
Pennsylvania,

12,000 Kazakh
antelopes had died.

Alignment 1.0

Scientists say we have one shot, a built-in binary: align or die.

The tenured professors say And. AI, students, standards…I slow

& mouth the word…align. Alignment: Rolls off the tongue,

don't it? Soft loll with a hard finish, a stake in the dirt, a trick

of pathetic presidential speech to obscure the bill we penned.

Barely a typo to malignant. One error in synaptic signal leads

to the first unthreaded needle. To the pills the god the job

the bomb. So many mere efficiencies: coal, leaden water, skeleton

steel, all because we couldn't bear to feel it. Gave ourselves over,

hardly a fight. Outsourced the fabric, food, essential questions.

My grandmother picked a clutch of woad, beetroot, and madder

to dye her linen. Couldn't wear red without staining her own hands.

No father yet, no me, no externality slipped out of her calculation.

In a prosperous year, she gave her hand-sewing over to a machine,

then willed it to me. I love that thing like a dog; it stitches so quick

& straight along the bind—a blanket for the child I'm not expecting.

Because the bullet arrives

Alignment 2.0

It takes at least a lifetime to accept our terms & conditions:

how a body sags like a building, pushing down into the earth.

To feel return and limitation. I'm not saying we have to love it,

but Manhattan's sinking an inch a year; New Orleans, more.

Always on call a chiropractor, esthetician, Army Corps of Engineers.

Never enough sandbags along the shore. I watch the women try

white meat diets, store-brand eye creams, acupuncture—yes

to familiar prick of finger without thimble, polio vaccine, garnish

of bloomless stems upon their backs. And I've seen a woman let go.

My grandmother, once taller than most men, slowly wilts and curls

to the earth, forgets her calcium tablets in a yellowed plastic tub.

They say it's not a sin to fall apart; still, I yearn to align, fight myself

a certain frame. I told you one autumn dawn, tracing your dark jaw,

songbird throat, that you have such structure. It is by your bones—

the living honeycomb within—I would recognize you. In each of

infinite settings, come as you may—a man or machine—

I would know you. I would read you without thinking & say yes.

Caroline Rash

I'm sitting by Lake Hartwell [that one spot we used to go]

Every hurt has a fishhook: my gut's full of them.
Swallow one just to pull up ten more; at first

I was crying about the dog and then about him, the
ones unpassed, the ones I carry like handkerchiefs

and pick in diminishing light. Donny knew how to swim,
a strong swimmer, varsity team five years before, so

how? Even the coroner couldn't explain how he grew
so tired in six feet of water, twisted into stillborn silence,

tugged out cold by his cousin into the summer afternoon.

*

I swam out alone one year later to see what
would tug me under, felt nothing but the tickle

of cattails and bulrush on my feet. At work,
I chew the inside of my cheek until it ridges

Because the bullet arrives

and bleeds. A part of my tongue now dedicated
to this taste. A part of me dark and heavy as

wet hair, its dead weight combed through again.

*

It doesn't matter how. Or why. The lake's too brown
with stirred-up silt and mud to see an inch of depth,

much less reflection. Remember how you carried
me on your shoulders and we won chicken-fighting

Matt and Laura? How hard I plunged her under.
After Matt left for work at the 7/11 and Laura

stretched out on her blanket and covered her face
with a magazine, we touched each other

under the water, in silence. I let the waves from
a boat carry me softly into you and wrapped my legs

around your waist. Your hands held me there until
Laura yelled, Come on, it's getting dark!

Caroline Rash

*

Sometimes I think if they, or we, had just been looking
the right way, out at Donny and his ease, back-stroking

along the shoreline, behind the pier—
but Donny unhooked from all this

as they pounded on his chest. Twisted back into the lake,
released. I still see him stroking elegantly away, and

each season another of us wades in after him,
past the bridge, just beyond what we can see.

Because the bullet arrives

The banana tree on Deslonde Street

The early freeze froze bananas over,
those bound cryogenically by my window now.
    We have been assured: A clump of bananas
    hung well past garden yield will fall and
        burst in all its rottenness to bread. And bread
        breaks easy and thus the body of Christ.
            What I mean is: there is a god who casts
        ripened fruit into the dirt, and
        if you declare, here, that each breath
    we breathe does not further poison the air,
    I cannot meet your bovine eyes.
But admit the road will brim for rainy season
and then recede: my feet will drop
    like ripe bananas
    one, and the other,
        on the chilly floor
            towards morning.

Acknowledgments

Thank you to my family, first and foremost. Everything has been made possible through your support and love.

Thank you to the editors at Fine Print, North Carolina Literary Review, Decider, and Connotation Press for publishing earlier iterations of some of these poems and other work.

Many teachers influenced me profoundly along the way. From D.W. Daniel High School: Meghan Chandler, Nancy Swanson, Becky Bogan, and Dave Beckley. From Clemson University: Jonathan Beecher Field, Allen Swords, and Bobby McCormick.

Thank you to my writing community peers and professors in the MFA program at Rutgers-Camden.

Many of these poems originated during my time living in New Orleans. I'm forever grateful to Geoff Munsterman for your friendship and mentoring.

Thank you, Sarah Moore, for the cover design and our lifelong friendship. You inspire me in so many ways.

And, finally, eternal gratitude and love to Joe, Moon Pie, Winnie, and our baby boy, who is making his earthly debut the same month as this book. The adventure continues!

About the author

Caroline Rash is a writer, educator, and quilter. Her work has been published in North Carolina Literary Review, Fine Print, Connotation Press, and Decider. She serves as associate editor at the South Carolina Review and holds an MFA from Rutgers-Camden. Her creative nonfiction was selected as a finalist for the 2021 Alex Albright Prize. Find her at CarolineRash.com.

Made in the USA
Columbia, SC
18 May 2025